DEATH VALLEY
Ghost Towns

by Stanley W. Paher

Nevada Publications
Box 15444
Las Vegas, Nevada

Las Vegas artist Roy E. Purcell has roamed the deserts for years to find suitable subjects for his etchings. On the front cover of this book is "The Descent" which has its setting in Marble Canyon. On the back cover is "The Prospector". Both etchings are adaptations of Death Valley photographs taken in about 1906.

Printed in the United States of America

Library of Congress Card Number 72-97900

Nevada Publications
Box 15444
Las Vegas, Nevada 89114

Table of Contents

The towns are listed here alphabetically for easy reference. Throughout the book the towns are in a geographical sequence.

Acknowledgments

The constant encouragement of many desert friends and acquaintances was a real source of strength while writing this book. All assistance to this project cannot be mentioned because of space limitations. Gabriel Vogliotti took time from a busy life of writing and patiently edited the entire manuscript. E. I. Edwards, who wrote the Foreword, read the text twice and offered valuable suggestions that greatly improved the book. Dennis Casebier's research contributed to the story of Saratoga Springs. Deke Lowe told the author about modern Tecopa mining. Captain Ray Gibson, the last living Death Valley teamster, told colorful stories about life at the Tonopah & Tidewater Railroad stations mentioned in this book. Walter Knott related his experiences about a small revival at Calico about the time of World War I.

Helping with pictures were Dorothy Rogers and Raul Rodriguez of the United States Borax and Chemical Corporation; Dolores Nariman of the Title Insurance and Trust Company of Los Angeles; and Frank Ackerman of the National Park System at Death Valley. Mrs. H. H. Heisler graciously loaned me many rare Rhyolite views.

Both cover etchings are those of desert artist Roy E. Purcell; the interior sketches are his also. He along with Cliff Nakatani and K. C. Den-Dooven offered general technical assistance to the production of this book.

Other photo credits are as follows: (an "a" denotes a picture at the top of page; "b" and "c" are those in descending order. Numerals in parenthesis designate the quantity of pictures on the page.) Gary Allen, 39b; Bancroft Library, 8; California State Library, 37; Captain Ray Gibson, 13a, 16a, 36b, Harry Gower, 19.

Mrs. H. H. Heisler, 27(2), 28a, 30a, 31; Los Angeles County Museum, 22b, 28b, 32; National Park Service (Death Valley), 22a, 23a, 23b, 24, 29a, 34; Nevada State Museum, 30c; Mrs. Henrietta Revert Collection, 14; Las Vegas *Review Journal,* 29b, 39b; Title Insurance and Trust Company of Los Angeles, 42, 44(2), 46, inside back cover; Tonopah *Times-Bonanza,* 34; U.S. Borax and Chemical Corporation, 17a, 41(2), 45a; U.S. Geological Survey, inside front cover, 39c; University of Nevada (Reno), 16b, John Yount Collection, 21(2).

Foreword

One of Stanley Paher's favorite pastimes is to search out rare old historical photographs and use them to illustrate and vitalize his articles and books about the desert. His monumental production—NEVADA GHOST TOWNS AND MINING CAMPS, with its 700 early photographic plates, is a classic example of the brilliant results attendant upon this project.

In his present volume he again emphasizes this visual approach to his subject. We are given a graphic concept of these riotous old mining camps as they appeared in photographs actually taken during those brief but glamorous days of their attempted ascendancy toward fame and fortune.

This book is essentially a story of beginnings. Paher writes vividly of the creation of these towns of yesteryear, whose skeletal remains are hidden deep in obscure canyons or perched precariously on rugged mountain slopes along the approaches to Death Valley. All are accorded brief descriptive accounts of their origin, their flamboyant heyday, their catastrophic decline, and their ultimate retreat into ghost town status.

Significantly, the pleasure experienced in viewing these early photographs, and in reading the historical comment, does not represent the *total* benefit to be derived from this unusual book. There is still another appeal. The book generates a compelling challenge to every desert lover and arouses him to go out and see for himself these fascinating places. This is how it affects me. I have seen most of these beckoning ghosts of once flourishing towns and have come to know some of them intimately. By the same token, there are a few I have not seen. Paher's book nudges me with an irresistible urge to go out and see them, even if

the only thing left to identify them is the ground they once stood on. For although every vestige of the town itself may have vanished into time and space, I can at least stand where that town once stood, and trust my imagination and Stanley Paher's early photographs to reconstruct it for me.

Happily, the author is explicit in his directions that tell us how to locate all these exciting places he so capably describes. The towns are arranged so that they follow each other in tour sequence from Furnace Creek Ranch, Stove Pipe Wells Village, and other modern localities.

Special attention should be directed to the section of the book that relates specifically to the subject of desert travel—its perils, health factors, and pertinent comments on the subject of desert survival. This is a most important chapter. It should be read and re-read until its substance becomes a working tool for all desert travelers.

In one of his earlier books—*Northwestern Arizona Ghost Towns*—the author expresses a thought I would like to pass on to the readers of this present volume. He writes: "Tucked away in several canyons are the skeletal remains of abandoned mines and towns. Delight in making friends with these desert ghosts awaits the traveler who can discriminate between solitude and loneliness."

I am confident the true desert lover can accomplish this discrimination and establish camaraderie with "these desert ghosts."

November 1972   E. I. Edwards

Mr. Edwards has written eleven books on Death Valley and Southern California's desert country.

5

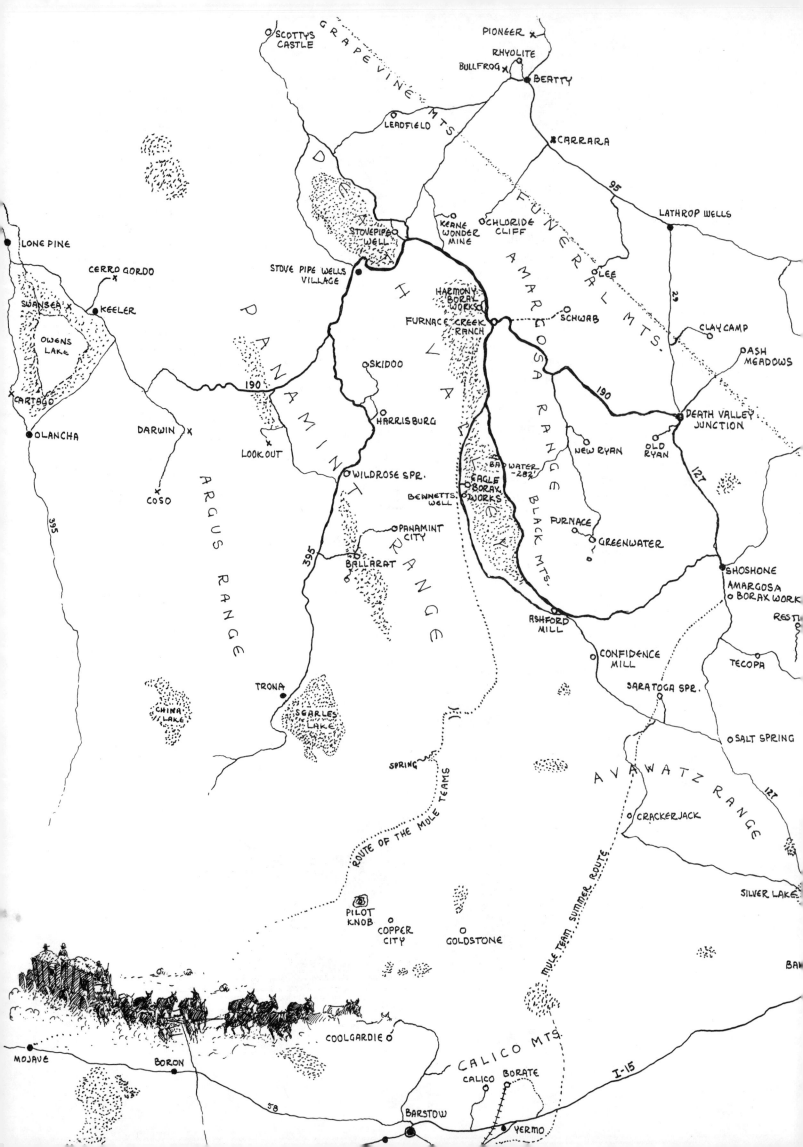

Death Valley Ghost Towns

FURNACE CREEK RANCH, 138 miles west of Las Vegas or 177 miles north of Barstow via Interstate-15.

Located below sea level in the midst of wide desolate Death Valley, Furnace Ranch initially was settled in 1870 by "Bellerin' Tex" Bennett, who wanted privacy. The spindly stream that flows through the ranch derived its name Furnace Creek from an event about ten years earlier, when a party of Mexican prospectors built a foot high assay furnace to use in determining whether recently gathered ore samples carried silver or lead.

In the early 1880's William T. Coleman, owner of the nearby Harmony Borax Works, bought the ranch to provide produce for his employees and hay for the animals. Cottonwood and palm trees were planted and alfalfa fields were laid out. In 1890 Francis M. "Borax" Smith took over the property, by then called the Greenland Ranch; it was at that time managed by the well-known Jimmy Dayton, who perished in 1899 while traveling on a wagon hitched to a six-horse team. He was enroute to the nearest supply point, Daggett, a town near Barstow. At the south end of the valley he sought refuge in the shade of a bush and died when overcome by the heat, leaving his horses standing in their harness to meet a similar fate.

After the turn of the century the ranch saw increased activity. The southern Nevada mining boom, which began at Tonopah in the spring of 1900 and reached Goldfield in the fall of 1902, worked its way to Rhyolite, adjacent to Death Valley, in the summer of 1904. Prospectors then combed the mountain ranges surrounding Death Valley, and the Greenland Ranch provided fresh food and a resting place for dozens of tired desert travelers. By the late 1920's some of the fenced acres grew alfalfa for the cattle that were later slaughtered to supply beef for miners working at nearby Ryan. The tamarisk-shaded bungalows still standing at the ranch were built in the early 1930's to accommodate the increasing number of Death Valley tourists and sightseers who could not afford the luxuries of nearby Furnace Creek Inn, built in 1927.

Furnace Creek Ranch has several points of interest. Near its entrance is the famous steam tractor "Old Dinah". A wagon train with its indispensable "tail-ender" or water wagon and locomotive number two of the Death Valley Railroad are also on display. At the Borax Museum and the adjacent National Park Visitor Center are mementos and numerous exhibits depicting the many faces of Death Valley.

HARMONY BORAX WORKS, immediately west of State Route 190 at a point 1.5 miles north of Furnace Creek Ranch.

In the winter of 1882, William T. Coleman built a borax mill near the foot of a low hill at the edge of a long dry white marsh where Aaron Winters of Ash Meadows (see page 18) had found borax cottonballs. Coleman organized the Harmony Borax Mining Company to carry out borax mining. In all, the settlement consisted of several adobe and stone buildings, a wooden warehouse, offices and stables.

From the crusty valley floor, an army of Chinese workmen gathered impure chunks of minerals from pin-head size to balls ten or twelve inches in diameter. They were loaded onto one-horse carts and hauled to the works.

Fortunately, the soft cottonballs required no crushing before being processed into borax crystals. The millhands dumped the minerals into tanks which contained water piped from a nearby spring. Crude carbonated soda mined from a nearby mesa also was added. The boiler was fired from underneath by varied local growth, especially the gnarled mesquite, a hard desert wood. Indian woodcutters gathered it from the area and piled it in huge stacks at the works.

A new chemical combination formed when the cottonballs, water and soda were heated to a boil and mixed. The solution was drawn off for crystallization in one of 35 covered tanks into which stout wires or rods were suspended. As the solution cooled, the refined borax accumulated as crystals on the rods which, once removed, looked like sticks of rock candy. A tap of a hammer knocked off the crystals. They were allowed to pile up and dry before being sacked for shipment.

The borax sacks were hauled to market by teams of eight to twelve mules and by the famous strings of twenty mule teams which usually consisted of two "wheeler" horses and eighteen mules. Two desert men handled each outfit—a swamper who watered and cared for the horses when not preparing meals, and the driver, an expert in line-jerking and profanity. Each team pulled two huge high-wheeled borax wagons and a water tank wagon. A rig averaged fifteen to twenty miles a day as it moved south and west to the railhead at Mojave, 165 agonizing miles over bleak deserts. The tough teamsters contended with sandstorms, maneuvered over sand and gravel, boulders and chuck-holes, and labored up and down steep mountain grades to complete the delivery of borax to a waiting box car. The round trip usually took a little more than three weeks, including a couple of days for layover in the shanties at Mojave for the teamster and swamper to enjoy faro and whiskey.

The Harmony works shut down each summer when temperatures rose above 115 degrees, because heat disturbed the refining process (see page 18). Major operations continued until 1888, when the price of borax fell, chiefly because of foreign imports. W. T. Coleman's company failed, though limited mining may have taken place in the following year. In March 1890 the property was acquired by "Borax" Smith, who thereafter held it merely as future reserve, because his operations at Borate (see page 43) by then had displaced all Death Valley producers. Smith consolidated his holdings in September 1890 into the Pacific Coast Borax Company, one of the predecessors of today's United States Borax & Chemical Corporation. The fenced-in rusted hulks of boilers are left, as well as a vat and adobe walls. Piles of borax remain out in the flats.

SCHWAB, 13 miles east of the Furnace Creek Ranch via State Route 190 and a steep and winding jeep road and trail.

Named in honor of Charles M. Schwab, president of Bethlehem Steel Corporation and a heavy investor in Rhyolite mines, the camp of Schwab in the midst of Echo Canyon was owned and promoted entirely by three women. Miss Fesler, a "blue-eyed blond with pretty teeth and a charming smile" and two married women "who were eager to colonize and increase the population" formed the Schwab Townsite Company in January 1907. They issued 30,000 shares at a dollar each, and men were reportedly eager purchasers. By March the camp had 200 people, including the usual floaters, and boasted a post office, a store, a restaurant, and a daily stage to Rhyolite. Before a newspaper could be brought in and a telephone line completed to the camp, the district folded that same summer. More recent production in Echo Canyon centered at the Inyo mine. Foundations mark the site.

America's most remote industrial plant in 1885 and Death Valley's first successful mill was the Harmony Borax Works. The partly exposed adobe-wood structure contains the huge boiler; five covered tanks also are shown. Their wide bottoms aided in the borax crystallization process. A twenty mule team carrying about half the capacity of a box car is ready to strike out for Mojave. From there the iron horse took the borax to market.

KEANE WONDER MINE, 9 miles north of State Route 190 at a point 11 miles north of Furnace Creek Ranch or 14 miles east of Stove Pipe Wells Village. The road is improved dirt the last three miles.

At this point which is 2500 feet above the floor of Death Valley and on the west slope of the Funeral Mountains, two veteran prospectors in 1903 staked claims to ore bodies later named the Keane Wonder mine. Beginning in 1908, the Keane Wonder Gold Mining Company stepped up operations. The height of activity was from June 1912 until the summer of 1914, when a post office operated here. But when developed ore bodies gave out in the spring of 1916, both mine and mill were closed down. Mining revived in the 1930's, and from that effort remain the ruins of crushers, a ball mill and ore bins. Production is said to have been valued at about $750,000.

EAGLE BORAX WORKS, 12.5 miles southwest of the paved Badwater Road at a point 6 miles south of Furnace Creek Ranch.

Isadore Daunet, lately of Panamint City and on his way to Arizona, discovered some mineral-ized "white lumps" a few miles north of Bennett's Well in 1875. When news circulated in 1881 that Aaron Winters had located borax a few miles north of Furnace Creek, the Frenchman recalled his earlier experience and enlisted partners to locate 270 acres of borax near Bennetts Well, 22 miles south of Furnace Creek. The men organized the Eagle Borax Company to mine the deposit, and immediately ordered equipment hauled across the Sierra Nevada. Once assembled, the primitive works consisted of a 22 foot long open boiler used to dissolve the impure borax crust and a dozen 1000 gallon tanks for crystallization. The mill was a Death Valley first.

In the years 1882 and 1883 Daunet shipped 260,000 pounds of borax to Daggett on the new Atlantic & Pacific Railroad. But competition from W. T. Coleman's Harmony and Amargosa operations, impure shipments, and problems from the summer heat all contributed to continual losses, and the two-year-old works was abandoned. Late in 1883 Coleman bought it to keep it from falling into competitive hands. Foundations and un-processed heaps of cottonball mark the site.

At a 3000 foot altitude, amid the somber grey-brown hills of the Funeral Mountains, the Keane Wonder mill with twenty stamps began to function in 1908. On top of the hill at right are towers of a 1400 foot tramway which sent gold-bearing ore directly into the mill which also had a cyanide plant to treat the tailings. In the foreground are bunkhouses.

GREENWATER, 1.5 miles west of the Furnace Creek-Shoshone road at a point 13.5 miles south of its junction with State Route 190.

The few residents in the Death Valley area late in the 19th century knew there was ore on the east slope of the Black Mountains and many alkali-stained prospectors had found minerals before 1900. However no mining development got underway because investors found the area so difficult to visit, a place lacking in water and food, reachable only with burros and animal-driven wagons.

The discovery of fantastically rich green-stained ore outcroppings that assayed up to 18% copper late in 1904 and early 1905 prompted grub-staker Arthur Kunze and others to open up the district in earnest in February 1906. Ultimately its magic lured a Who's Who of big-time national investors, including such men as industrialists Charles Schwab and John Brock of Pennsylvania, copper magnates William Clark of Montana and "Patsy" Clark of Washington State, and Tasker Oddie of Nevada—then superintendent and part owner of the rich Mizpah mine at Tonopah and later to be a Nevada Senator and Governor.

Kunze and a promoter named Ramsey each platted a townsite; Clark founded the town of Furnace as an unsuccessful rival. In 1906-1907 dozens of mining companies sold stock to a gullible public caught up in the mining excitement brought about by the authentic values of Goldfield securities. Many believed that a fortune could be made simply by investing in property owned by (or adjacent to) those of the big names already there.

Talented shysters were happy to relieve the unwary of their savings. Many filed claims on land whether it was mineralized or not. They incorporated companies with the word "Greenwater" in them, capitalized them from $1 million to $5 million, and promoted their stock with tantalizing literature showing Greenwater as another Butte. The first issue of *Copper Talk* proclaimed Greenwater a record breaker with "mammoth ledges and astounding values. . . . There can be but one future for Greenwater, and that will be expressed by the six words, 'Greatest Copper Camp in the World.' "

The many Greenwater shares were traded furiously, especially in the big Eastern exchanges. The most noted of the fast-buck artists, George Graham Rice, estimated that the public invested $30 million here in less than four months. Green-water & Death Valley Mining Company stock, originally capitalized at three million shares with a par value of $1, and underwritten by New York and Pittsburg stock exchange members, reached almost $5.50 a share on the New York curb. This meant a paper valuation of $16.5 million. Another company, the United Greenwater, sold more than 150,000 shares at $1, only to see the price soar to $2.50. These two companies merged to form the Greenwater Copper Mines & Smelters Company, with a capitalization of $25 million with five million shares at $5 par value. Sales were brisk, even though the company owned no ore-bearing veins whatsoever.

By early 1907 the Greenwater district had about a thousand people from all walks of life—especially speculators, merchants, promoters, laborers, prostitutes (Diamond-toothed Lil's place was conveniently located next to the post office), and many serious miners who searched underground for elusive rich copper veins. All felt discovery of the big ore body was imminent—tomorrow!

In 1907 most people moved out of the Kunze townsite which was in a cramped gulch, to the Ramsey location two miles southeast and on a broad slope large enough to allow for a city of 100,000. In spirit, Greenwater was that already. In 1907 it boasted many stores, a post office, and competing weeklies—the *Times* and the *Miner*.

Desert drivers made hair raising auto stage runs to and from Rhyolite, and the vehicles of "Alkali Bill" Brong's fast running "Death Valley Chug Wagon" made daily connections with T. & T. and Las Vegas & Tonopah railroad stations. More than 2500 mining claims were staked along the Funeral Range running 15 miles north and south of town, along what promoters called the great Greenwater mineral belt.

The semi-monthly men's magazine, the *Death Valley Chuck-Walla*, was published, "mixing the dope cool from the mountains and hot from the desert." It cost only ten cents a copy. Wood ran $60 a cord, hay came to $6 or $7 a bale, and gasoline a dollar a gallon. Ice from Las Vegas cost $10 for 100 pounds. A loaf of bread sold for a quarter. Ham 'ands were never cheaper than a dollar a plate. Water hauled from the Amargosa River, forty miles away, was scarce at $7.50 to $15 a barrel. (The editor of the Greenwater *Miner* watched his house go up in smoke because the water to put out the flames would have cost more than the house was worth.)

In 1906 the Kunze Greenwater townsite had a scattering of tents that housed saloons, the post office and the office and the press of the Greenwater Times, a weekly booster of the camp. In the bottom view, note the burros with the packsaddles and the men with picks, shovels and surveying instruments. Greenwater with its strong speculative backing had all the trimmings of a successful mining camp except for ore.

Flamboyant advertising (opposite page) lured millions of dollars to Greenwater for investment in stocks and real estate at this supposedly rich copper district. A gullible public snatched up issues of stock as fast as certificates came from the press.

The usual false fronted buildings (above) lined Greenwater's main street which was laid out extra wide as a fire break. Before a paying mine was developed, Greenwater had a $100,000 bank, an office of the Tonopah & Tidewater Railroad, offices of professional men, and the usual saloons to ward off thirst in that dry country. The best way to get to Greenwater was by "Alkali Bill" Brong's crowded auto stages. He was the premier desert chauffeur of the Death Valley country. Big horse teams (below) brought in all freight because no railroad ever was built to the district. The hauls were expensive, since water barrels and feed consumed valuable wagon space. Greenwater's great outlays of money for development, small returns, and quick decline had few parallels in mining annals.

EIGHTEEN HORSE TEAM

Greenwater boosters spoke of building a $2 million copper smelter near Ash Meadows to treat local ores and talked of extending short lines about the district, but the decline came in the fall of 1907, when copper could not be found in commercial quantities. This along with the start of the national money panic brought about Greenwater's fast demise. Paper fortunes evaporated and the market value of stocks fell even faster than they had risen, closing a chapter in one of history's monumental stock fiascos. The post office was discontinued the following spring, 1908, and virtually no mining took place thereafter. The site of Greenwater has caved-in cellars and a few graves, while at the Kunze townsite are a few wooden buildings amid vast piles of broken glass.

FURNACE, 3.5 miles north-northwest of Greenwater, via unimproved roads.

One of the original towns in the Greenwater district was Furnace, the camp of the Furnace Creek Copper Company, whose principal backer was "Patsy" Clark. In early 1907 the one-year-old town consisted chiefly of tent buildings, with a store, a restaurant, a post office and a saloon serving the miners working on nearby copper veins. Speculation over company shares ran the stock up to more than $5 a share on the New York curb. But the Furnace Townsite Company produced only stock certificates rather than copper ore, and Furnace town died when nearby Greenwater collapsed, late in 1907. Some dugouts, wooden debris, and a collapsed gallows frame mark the site.

RYAN (New Ryan), 4 miles south of State Route 190 at a point 12 miles south of Furnace Creek Ranch or 18 miles west of Death Valley Junction.

Even before the Lila C. mine played out at old Ryan in 1914, the Pacific Coast Borax Company had decided to relocate its mining operations at the Biddy McCarthy, the Widow mine and other adjacent properties at the present site of Ryan. The company built the 17 mile long narrow-gauge Death Valley Railroad from here to its new concentrating mill at Death Valley Junction.

During the next year the transfer of operations (including removal of the post office) from the older Ryan was completed, and beginning early in 1916 the company began shipping borax. From the Widow mine gasoline trains operating on two-foot (baby-gauge) rails hauled ore from the mines for seven winding miles and through a series of tunnels to storage bins at Ryan. From here the DV RR took the ore directly to the mill.

By 1927 the population reached as much as 250 when operations closed down in favor of a newly discovered borax deposit at Boron in Kern County, a find both more extensive and more accessible. It became an open pit operation. The Ryan post office closed early in 1930. Until that year the borax company unsuccessfully maintained the Death Valley View Hotel as a resort, though sightseeing tours on the baby-gauge continued until about 1950. Several guarded houses and mine buildings are left.

At an altitude of 2000 feet, Ryan was a modern company town of the 1920's. The rows of modern houses contained a complete sanitary system, and the borax company also installed hoists and gasoline speeders to replace mule power at the mines. Recreational facilities included weekly movies, tennis courts, and a swimming pool. It is said that the camp's social hall was a former church that had been hauled in from Rhyolite. Brilliant streaks of rose, fawn and milky green blemish the rugged slopes of the Black Mountains.

AMARGOSA HOTEL, DEATH VALLEY JCT. CALIF. FRASHERS FOTO

Death Valley Junction bustled during the 1920's while borax was being shipped from nearby Ryan. By the late 1930's the town concerned itself with refining filter clay. The famed Amargosa Hotel is the large building in the center of the picture, while the Funeral Range dominates the background. Some of the machinery in the borax mill (below) was in the concentrator at the camp of old Ryan, shown on the opposite page. Mill buildings are at left. Shaft structures indicate the location of two of the five shafts at Ryan.

16

DEATH VALLEY JUNCTION, at the junction of State Routes 127 and 190; 109 miles northwest of Las Vegas or 147 miles northeast of Barstow via Interstate-15.

This community came into being early in the summer of 1907 as a telegraph station on the Tonopah & Tidewater Railroad, then being built from Ludlow, California northward to Beatty, Nevada. In August of that same year a spur was built from here to the Lila C. borax mine at Ryan, seven miles southwest. The new junction town soon acquired a tent hotel, a saloon, and a store operated by Bob Tubbs. From here passengers headed for Death Valley caught stages.

After the concentrator was removed from old Ryan in 1915, Death Valley Junction grew into a lively community with additional stores, a school, a boarding house and eventually fireproof dormitories for millhands. Several houses were moved in from old Ryan and Greenwater, as well as from Rhyolite. It became the "metropolis" and social center for the area east of Death Valley. Movies and dancing to live music were favorite pastimes.

The huge $400,000 concentration mill handled only second class ore from new Ryan; the best was shipped by railroads directly to refineries at Alameda, California and Bayonne, New Jersey. When mining at Ryan ceased in 1927, Death Valley Junction continued to thrive, even though the mill shut down. By then tourists were coming in increasing numbers, especially after Death Valley National Monument was created in 1933; and the Amargosa Hotel with a pillared 300-foot veranda welcomed many visitors.

Throughout the 1930's service on the T & T slowed, and weekly trains discharged few passengers and very little freight. In June 1940 the railroad ceased running. Since then nearby farms and ranches and towns have kept the community alive. In 1971 a new 150,000-ton borax mill built north of here just inside the Nevada state line began to treat ore mined seven miles to the west, below old Ryan. Population at Death Valley Junction is now at about fifty. Here it is possible to go to the ballet at the Amargosa Opera House.

RYAN (Old Ryan), via unimproved dirt road 5.5 miles southwest of State Route 127 at a point 1.5 miles south of Death Valley Junction.

With the gradual depletion of borax deposits at Borate early in this century, the Pacific Coast Borax Company had to look elsewhere for uninterrupted production. The company already owned the Lila C. mine, discovered as early as 1882, but transporting the mineral from such an inaccessible spot was prohibitive.

Nevertheless in 1903 the company shifted its main operations to the Lila C. Three years later the Tonopah & Tidewater laid rails to nearby Death Valley Junction, and in the fall of 1907 a seven mile branch line was extended to the camp. Iron horses then replaced forever the spectacular twenty mule teams which thereafter served only in borax company publicity work, including tours down boulevards of large eastern cities.

From 1907 through 1914, the period when the Lila C. produced continuously, Ryan had a few hundred people and a small post office. The camp offered little recreation other than a poorly equipped reading room, but eleven of the men did organize the Death Valley brass band. After 1914 operations went to New Ryan, twelve miles northwest, and the concentrator that operated here was moved to Death Valley Junction. All structures have been removed; only white patches of tailings mark the site.

ASH MEADOWS, 8 miles northeast of Death Valley Junction via improved dirt road.

For many centuries Indians had roamed this area, providing the first instance of human activity, and in 1849 one party of westbound emigrants stopped here to rest and dip their buckets into the area's several waterholes. At various times Shoshones also made camps for extended periods and saw both Jacob Breyfogle (of the lost mine fame) in 1864 and Lieutenant George Wheeler's survey party in 1871 pass by. Occasional desert prospectors also came; and Ash Meadows, named for the tough-leafed ash trees that grow in the area, was so remote that from time to time it served ideally as an outlaw refuge.

Early in the 1880's, Aaron and Rosie Winters lived near one of the springs in a combination dugout and shack made of wood and stone with a dirt floor. When a stranger passed by showing specimens of a hard white substance he called borax, Winters remembered seeing the mineral in the wide playa below Furnace Creek. After gathering samples and successfully testing them, he turned to his dark-eyed, black-haired wife and exclaimed, "She burns green, Rosie!" He then staked several claims and soon sold them to William Coleman for a reported $20,000, thus starting a borax boom in Death Valley.

After 1905 "Dad" Fairbanks operated an important stage stop on the road to Bullfrog from the Salt Lake Route railroad stations at Ivanpah and at the new town of Las Vegas, each more than sixty miles south. Overnight accommodations were available for both men and animals in very airy bedrooms with a star-lit sky as the ceiling. A large tent saloon quenched alkali-coated throats. Meals boarding house style cost fifty cents.

After World War I non-metallic minerals—clay and potash—were gathered profitably. By 1923 a rude collection of tents, tin shacks and dugouts seven miles northwest of Ash Meadows took the name Clay Camp, where a large reduction plant processed and dried the wet clay. Three years later the Death Valley Railroad built a four mile spur from a Tonopah & Tidewater siding to service the pits at Clay Camp. The valley also provided a safe retreat for bootleggers, and Clay Camp had an elementary school for its several dozen inhabitants. By 1932 virtually all mining ceased. Ash Meadows became a small ranching community and now is a small tree-shaded resort. Of Clay Camp only concrete ruins and clay pits are left to indicate the site.

AMARGOSA BORAX WORKS, on the east side of State Route 127 at a point 5.5 miles south of Shoshone.

Borax discoveries at this point near the Amargosa River in 1882 proved to be valuable for William Coleman, owner of Harmony Borax Works (see page 7). Early summer temperatures that reached 120 degrees and more on the floor of Death Valley did not permit borax refining there, even when workers played a water hose over the felt carpets that covered the crystallizing vats.

To counter the summer layoff at Harmony, Coleman purchased this deposit in 1883 for $15,000 and ultimately organized the Meridian Borax Mining Company. In late spring when the thermometer at the Harmony plant began to rise above 115 degrees, Coleman moved his crews here where mid-summer temperatures seldom rose above a more workable 110 degrees. With this second operation, Coleman maintained uninterrupted borax shipments during 1883-1888. Throughout each summer jerkline mule teams hauled the product from these works 135 miles to the nearest railroad station, Daggett, where the borax was transferred into waiting box cars of the Atlantic & Pacific Railroad.

Borax mining and processing stopped here permanently after the summer of 1887 and the plant was dismantled. In 1907, when the Tonopah & Tidewater Railroad was built east of here, the station took the name Zabriskie, after an important borax official. It served as a temporary railhead for the booming Greenwater district until the T. & T. ran farther north. Zabriskie became a small trading center that after August 1907 had a post office as well. The community died when the neighboring station of Shoshone became the area's trading center. The post office was discontinued in 1918. Adobe walls and foundations mark the site of the borax works.

TECOPA, 10 miles south of Shoshone via State Route 127 and Tecopa Road.

The district's principal mine, the Gunsight, was discovered in 1865. Work soon got underway and a smelter, erected a few years later, began treating the lead-silver ores. In the mid-1870's the Los Angeles Mining & Smelting Company stepped up development work by purchasing the Gunsight and the nearby Noonday mine and built furnaces. By the spring of 1877 most people in the district moved to Tecopa from the original camp at a large spring close to the Noonday mine.

Resting Springs in the Tecopa district was a rest stop on the Spanish Trail in the 1830's and 1840's and later became the site of a settlement and at least one mill. This picture was taken just before 1900.

For the next four years or so, no one knew whether Inyo or San Bernardino county should collect the taxes in the new town. From the time of its opening in May 1877, the Tecopa post office changed counties three times until 1881, when a boundary survey determined that the village was four miles within Inyo County. But mining and smelting operations in the late 1870's proved to be slow and unproductive, and the local furnaces were abandoned after running only about a year. Charcoal for the furnaces had to be hauled forty miles from kilns in Wheeler Wash, on the west side of the Spring Mountains west of Las Vegas.

Early in 1879 a pulverizing mill began operating at Resting Spring. After it failed another 10-stamp mill was built that same summer. It also could not make the ore pay and by 1880 all milling stopped. In the next year a San Francisco mining engineer ran a 1000 foot tunnel to cut the lode at lower levels and help eliminate costly hoisting; but when the lode was reached in 1881 the ore proved to be too poor to work profitably and the mines closed. Tecopa's residents moved on to fairer ground and the post office was removed in the fall of 1881.

The district revived in May 1907 when the Tonopah & Tidewater Railroad was built through Tecopa. The mines reopened briefly eleven months later. Early in 1910 the Tecopa Consolidated Mining Company completed construction of the 9.5 mile long Tecopa Railroad from Te-copa to the Gunsight and Noonday mines and worked them irregularly until 1928, shipping about $3 million in lead-silver ores especially to Murray, Utah for smelting. During most of the 1940's the Anaconda Mining Company operated these mines and equalled the earlier outputs. Since then the mines have been quiet most years, though new work started in the early 1970's. A small population makes a living from the tourist and hot springs resort trade. An old railroad grade, mine and smelter ruins are east of town.

ASHFORD MILL, on the west side of the paved Badwater Road at a point 28 miles west of Shoshone or 44.5 miles south of Furnace Creek Ranch.

Perched high on the Black Mountains three miles to the east is the Ashford (or Golden Treasure) mine, initially located in 1907. When it began to show some high-grade and broad veins of workable quality, the owners decided to build a mill on the pale brush-dotted floor of Death Valley. Gravel was found nearby and a carload of concrete was purchased, but the cement company mistakenly shipped a double order. Thus when the mill and associated buildings were constructed in 1915 they had extra thick walls. Unfortunately, inefficient operations forced a shutdown after the mill had treated only a few tons of ore. Subsequent litigation also complicated mining. Massive concrete foundations and a tailings pile mark the site. A steep road ending as a rock trail leads to the mine portal.

19

CONFIDENCE MILL, 9 miles by improved road south of Ashford Mill.

Some have written that, around 1855 or before, Mormons were operating here, but this is extremely doubtful. Just who conducted the first mining operation here has not been determined. A cyanide plant operated unsuccessfully around 1909, and later a nearby 2400 acre bed of nitre, a type of salt, was unenthusiastically worked. Foundations and a pit remain at Confidence Mill.

SARATOGA SPRINGS, 25.5 miles south of Ashford Mill by imroved dirt road, then three miles north by unimproved dirt road.

Initially these 25 foot wide springs at the extreme southern end of Death Valley were a camping spot for early expeditions. As early as 1860, Lieutenant B. F. Davis of the First Dragoons of the U. S. Army stopped here with his command enroute to Death Valley in search of Indians. The men marched north to near Bennetts Well before turning back after finding no Indians.

In this century the nearby hills were investigated for deposits of nitre and other salts. Near the springs several tents and a few stores rose beside an old dugout that was built in the 19th century. Around 1930 one firm bottled mineral water from here. The dugout and some debris mark the site.

SALT SPRINGS, .5 mile east of State Route 127 at a point 28 miles south of Shoshone or 29 miles north of Baker.

This locality has had a varied history. In the early 1830's pack trains traveling the Spanish Trail from New Mexico to southern California began stopping here, continuing until that activity ceased in 1848. Four years earlier, Western pathfinder John C. Fremont described this camp ground as a swampy, salty spot with only poor grass. Under the able leadership of the desert guide Jefferson Hunt, a Mormon caravan bound for California rested at the brackish water. Some in that party found gold-bearing rock near the spring. Samples were gathered and later displayed in Los Angeles. This was eastern California's first recorded discovery of precious minerals.

Early in 1850 work commenced at the "Mormon Diggings," as they were first called. In 1851 two companies mined the ore and worked it in local arrastras, but the location proved to be too remote to work profitably. People living here in the late 1850's and early 1860's organized the Salt Springs mining district to exploit the "Amargoza"

mines. They were on the heavily traveled Salt Lake-Los Angeles "Mormon Trail," which food-begging Indians also passed over. This early effort was short lived because of extreme isolation and Indian depredations, which involved the burning of a mill. When Lieutenant George Wheeler came to this deserted camp in 1871, he noted many abandoned buildings, adits and stump heads, showing that the mines by that time had been worked considerably.

New owners in the 1880's set up machinery and recovered some gold. Early in this century another experienced mine owner profitably worked the district, using a 5-stamp mill, and for most years since then a few individuals occasionally have shipped ore. Foundations and tailings mark the site.

SILVER LAKE, alongside State Route 127 at a point 8.5 miles north of Baker.

After the Tonopah & Tidewater laid rails through here early in 1906, Silver Lake sprang up as the railroad town that served as a supply point for the mines in the surrounding mountains and for Crackerjack and Copper City. The Rose, Heath, Fisk Company annually sold about $150,000 in goods and supplies, and in conjunction operated a considerable stage business. This town of about 100 people also had boarding houses, saloons, a depot with a telegraph office and, as of March 1907, a post office.

In August 1908 a flood submerged several miles of T. & T. track north of town, and dull times prevailed until it was repaired. When a similar tragedy hit in January 1916, flooding the town itself, Silver Lake was relocated a little to the east. By the 1920's most businesses had departed and in 1933 the post office was moved to nearby Baker. Silver Lake became a ghost town soon after the T. & T. stopped running in 1939. Scattered ties and some adobe walls are left.

CRACKERJACK, 25 miles west of Silver Lake, by primitive roads.

Gold discoveries in 1906, two miles southwest of Cave Spring below Avawatz Pass, sparked a mild boom and the birth of a camp which soon had tent saloons and stores. A post office began operating after February 1907. Regularly scheduled auto and horse-drawn stages shuttled mine boomers from the nearest railroad point, Silver Lake, and from Daggett. Mining lasted only about two years and only mine ruins remain of Crackerjack.

In 1906 the village of Silver Lake bustled as a railhead while the Tonopah & Tidewater Railroad was laying tracks on the floor of the dry bed of Silver Lake, just north of town. Even after trains began running to stations along the line farther north, passenger traffic kept the town lively. The principal business was in the above building. Beneath the roof of the porch is a rolled up canvas awning that was unraveled late each afternoon. Many of the residences (below) which were scattered about the town were cared for by women who came to the desert while their husbands or fathers worked locally or mined gold and silver in the surrounding hills. Water haulers drove their wagons beneath the elevated water outlet near the gate to fill their barrels.

There he goes, with his overalls or corduroys covered with dust and grease. His whiskers are ragged and he has a hungry look. He tells fantastic stories of easily acquired riches and preaches a gospel of faith, hope and works. Occasionally he possesses a college sheepskin but more often he is uneducated, though versatile in lying about his finds. He searches endlessly for leads, almost freezing to death in winter, with only canvas and bacon and the silvery vision of the future to ease the burden of primitive surroundings. Barren deserts, Indians, chilling snows, scorching sands, hunger, thirst—none of these stops him.

At left a prospector with his two jacks heads out across the desert toward Bullfrog. His worldly goods consist of little more than a pipe, a cooking utensil, a few canteens, whiskey and grub, tools, a blanket, an old sheepskin jacket, and a change of clothing. When prospectors were in camp (below), they talked like millionaires, planning mills and laying out streets and railroads as if such things were mere incidents in a day's work. Actually, most were chronically poor and died alone in the mountains or sank out of sight in the smoky corner of a saloon.

The Prospector

Prospectors (above) are recovering gold by swirling ore-bearing particles and water in an ordinary gold pan, a large steel dish usually about a foot in diameter. By this method, water and lighter unprofitable gravel were cast off, while the heavier gold particles, "colors," rimmed the pan.

Early in this century the cost of burros leaped with the value of mining stocks. Burros were a reliable source of entertainment besides being essential to carrying provisions and gear (shown strewn about the camp) on packsaddles. The wandering prospectors and burros heard only the call of the wild. After only a day or two spent locating claims in one locality, the men with their pack trains would be off again—nobody knew for where —often with hardly enough supplies to last them back to the settlements. It did not matter if they discovered a good thing—say a nest of ledges worth a thousand apiece. They were constantly looking for something better.

Cradled between two towering mountain ranges wrinkled and streaked with vivid shades of brown and rosy tan, is the famous Death Valley. This vast treeless alkali plain extends north and south for about 130 miles and averages about a dozen miles in width. It is the lowest, hottest and driest place in North America. Temperatures annually rise to more than 130 degrees. The Indians named this gristly playa, Tomesha—ground afire.

Ever since California-bound emigrants traversed this dazzling white valley in 1849, exaggerated tales of blazing temperatures and hidden riches have come from here. Apocryphal stories tell of dozens and even hundreds of animals and emigrant men and women dying in the valley. Actually, only one human perished here in 1849-1850. Moreover, the "49ers" did not lose their way in coming to Death Valley, as many have written. The emigrants organized themselves near Provo, Utah in October 1849 to plan a southwestern course under the able leadership of Mormon guide, Jefferson Hunt. But early in November at a point near modern Enterprise, Utah, many of the emigrants defected in favor of striking directly westward over raw deserts over a "middle route" to California through Walker Pass. If successful, they would save more than 500 miles by not traveling Hunt's southern route.

The emigrants soon splintered into many small groups. Some defectors turned back to rejoin Hunt. But during November and December 1849 about a hundred men and women plodded westward from waterhole to waterhole, though fully conscious of moving westward to central California. Upon entering the salty waste of Death Valley, the several groups found themselves baffled and walled in by the lofty snow-capped Panamint Range which towers more than two miles above the valley floor. In hapless attempts to cross that barrier, the Jayhawker group was stalled a full week. But the Bennett-Arcane party had to endure the Valley for five terrifying weeks while awaiting rescue by William Manly and Rogers. After reaching civilization, individuals in the various groups told dire stories of their misfortunes. Rumors exaggerated their plight and added stories of hidden riches in Death Valley and in the surrounding mountains.

After those days of '49, only a few intrepid prospectors penetrated the area in search of minerals. Finally in the early 1860's various companies and individuals mined gold and silver in some districts, but no sustained boom got underway until Panamint in the 1870's. Finally it was borax early in the 1880's that put Death Valley on the map. Thereafter brave adventurers explored the area and discovered many springs which aided prospectors and travelers who ventured into the Death Valley country early in this century. Such important camps as Rhyolite, Skidoo, and Greenwater then were developed.

RHYOLITE, 1.5 miles north of State Route 58 at a point 4 miles west of Beatty. Paved roads throughout.

The remarkable early 20th century mineral discoveries at Tonopah and Goldfield stimulated prospecting throughout the Death Valley country after 1904. In August of that year, while punching their train of five burros to and from the Keane Wonder mine, Frank "Shorty" Harris and Eddie Cross located a prominent quartz outcrop at what soon became the Bullfrog claim. That name probably came from the ore's green color and from the irony of associating the lowly bullfrog with this arid place.

Beginning that very fall hundreds of prospectors and mining camp followers rushed to the Bullfrog hills, and numerous claims soon covered the mineralized ground between the Bullfrog mine and the Amargosa River, where the town of Beatty sprang up. Below the discovery site the village of Amargosa City rose complete with saloons, stores and an unofficial post office. Several other paper towns were platted in the sage before Pete Busch staked Rhyolite townsite amid the principal mines in a horseshoe-shaped draw between Ladd and Bonanza mountains.

In February 1905 the lure of free lots induced most people in the other canvas towns to build in Rhyolite. A red hot mining rush soon developed and the cry was "Bullfrog or Bust!" Footpackers, men trailing burros, saddle outfits, light rigs of every description, mule-driven freighters, and houses mounted on wagons all descended upon the district. Scores of autos came loaded with eager men who paid $25.00 to get here from Goldfield.

White canvas was spread daily during that spring and embryonic Rhyolite grew as if by magic. With one accord the butcher, the baker, the hasher, the banker and the druggist hung out signs and shingles. Innkeepers conducted business in tents stretched over a wooden frame with a bottom boxed for a few feet up on all sides. A bed was a dollar a night in a two-cot room with loosely hung curtains serving as interior walls.

The Rhyolite *Herald* began weekly publication in May 5, 1905, and the post office opened a fortnight later. Thereafter, Rhyolite's fame spread even more rapidly. The usual rainbow chasers were followed by nationally known moneyed men such as Charles Schwab, who bought the Montgomery-Shoshone mine and built a 200-ton mill. Promoters quickly advertised stock to raise money to begin mining development of several properties.

Sweat-stained mule and horse teams continually picked up supplies shipped by railroad to the new town of Las Vegas, while other teamsters brought in freshly cut lumber from Mount Charleston. Auto and horse stages whisked passengers from Ivanpah and Las Vegas to the new desert mining metropolis. The immense amount of traffic encouraged talk of railroad construction.

By early 1906 wood-frame and stone buildings began replacing the tents. Property values were on the rise, credit was good and money was plentiful. Telephone and telegraph wires were stretched across the desert. "Rhyolite is growing bigger and deeper every day," wrote one reporter. Some of the most optimistic compared the district's ore with the high-grade from Goldfield. The prominent mines were the Original Bullfrog, Denver, Montgomery Shoshone, Tramp, National Bank, and Steinway.

These mines survived the April 1906 San Francisco earthquake which seriously affected many other western mining operations. Only the richest ores were freighted to mills at Goldfield or hauled to Las Vegas for delivery to Salt Lake City smelters. Mine owners concentrated on developing their properties until November 1906 when the Las Vegas & Tonopah Railroad reached the district and began hauling out ore. By mid-1907 the Bullfrog Goldfield Railroad began running to the town. Three months later the Tonopah & Tidewater also competed for ore shipments out of the Bullfrog district.

During the height of the boom in 1907, Rhyolite's wide streets were constantly crowded with people going from brokerage to saloon, from cafe to real estate office. Newsboys peddled Denver, San Francisco and Salt Lake newspapers. Besides a thriving "red light" district that contained girls from San Francisco's Barbary Coast, there were churches, a bottling works, ice plants, a modern telephone exchange, an opera house, and even a symphony orchestra. Four competing newspapers and two locally printed magazines served this city of 6,000.

During the boom days of 1906-1907, fashion conscious women (top, opposite page) bought Collier's, Woman's Home Companion, *and* Elite Styles. *The well-dressed men about town stopped by the stock exchange at least every few hours for new returns. The telegraph kept this office in constant touch with exchanges at Goldfield, Tonopah and Reno.*

RHYOLITE STOCK EXCHANGE. OPENING DAY, MARCH 25, 1907.

Many of the first residents of Rhyolite arrived by auto stages. Early in this century the desert choked and seethed with the snorting and jerking of autos whirring across the dust-covered flats between the mining camps. Oil, extra gasoline, tires, axles and other spare parts had to be carried. In the middle view is one of the back streets of Rhyolite. Note the "powder room" in the left foreground. Home sweet home at the suburb of Bullfrog (bottom) meant tolerating the dust, flies, nosey burros and other animals. Despite the crude surroundings, the women could dress well when a photographer arrived.

At the Denver mine (above) high-grade ore is sacked awaiting shipment to the mill. Promoters sang the praises of the mines of the Bullfrog district, often making exaggerated claims of ore values. But it could not compare with the remarkable high-grade mined at Goldfield.

Situated on Bonanza Mountain, the Tramp Consolidated mine was a typically promoted Rhyolite enterprise. Its owners obtained controlling interest in the property for a mere $150,000, incorporated it by issuing two million shares with a par value of $1 each, and then boosted the mine by brazen claims of high values. By 1907 or 1908 the price of the stock had tripled on the New York curb. But in 1911 Tramp plummeted to only three cents a share and never had it paid a dividend. Recorded production was a mere 540 tons of ore.

These four buildings of Rhyolite's boom days still survive. The school (top) also was used for dances and lodge meetings. The $90,000 John S. Cook Bank had offices for professional men. Thousands of empty champagne and beer bottles were used in 1906 to build the bottle house. The fine mission style railroad depot was called the "Dearborn Street Station of the West."

JOHN S. COOK & CO.'S BANK, RHYOLITE, NEV.

A drilling contest was a very important part of a Rhyolite holiday celebration. Miners from throughout the area tested their skills in "double-hand" and "single-hand" contests. In the former, two men (as shown below) worked together—one struck the drill and the other held it and turned it after each blow. In the "single-hand" or one-man contest, the participant held, struck and turned the drill into a solid block or boulder. He won if he could drive a hole deeper than anyone else within a specified time. Betting was often heavy on the drillers, who worked even more enthusiastically when the crowd shouted or burst into patriotic songs. On this hot day (note the umbrellas) the spectators undoubtedly sought refuge in the saloons to satisfy thirst. A dance that evening would end the day of festivities.

The Porter Brother's store was doing a $150,000 per month gross business in general merchandise before the national financial panic of late 1907 finally caught up with the town. Smaller mines quickly folded and development work slowed. Wall Street money and credit which had built the town suddenly dried up. Its $20,000 school was filled to only a quarter of capacity. The 1910 census found 675 people, and by 1922 only a solitary Frenchman remained.

For many years thereafter Rhyolite's several dozen wooden and concrete buildings stood with books and other furnishings in place. Heavy mining equipment was left near crumbling walls. Total district production was a recorded $3.1 million from twelve mines.

In later years the expensive $90,000 LV & T railroad depot became a casino. This most substantial building of old Rhyolite is now a residence and souvenir shop. Ranking second in interest is the famous "Bottle House" built of thousands of beer discards. Golden Street, Rhyolite's main thoroughfare, has been reduced to pale stone and concrete skeletons. Many abandoned railroad grades run to important mines. At the lower end of the town is a cemetery.

While rambunctious Rhyolite thrived near the mines of the Bullfrog district, the tranquil town of Beatty grew up five miles east along the Amargosa River, a feeble rill of water fed by springs a few miles to the north. Small ranches near those water sources were havens for 19th century Death Valley prospectors who spent a night in more comfortable surroundings before again heading into the wilds. During 1905-1907 Beatty grew fast; enterprising saloon men opened more than a dozen establishments in false fronted buildings, as shown below. Inside, mustached capitalists sipped chilled beer with grizzly prospectors. Stagecoaches brought in ice until a local plant was built south of town in 1906. Since the buildings were decorated with the national colors, it was probably Independence Day. The blasting of dynamite and the shooting of guns provided noise, as firecrackers were banned because of fire danger.

LEADFIELD, 14.5 miles (on one-way road west-bound) west of State Route 58 at a point 6 miles west of Beatty.

In the early spring of 1926 the town of Lead-field came into boisterous being in the upper part of 11-mile long Titus Canyon, a colorful rugged defile that cuts and winds 5,500 feet through the Grapevine Mountains to the floor of Death Valley. The town was conceived by stock promoter and manipulator C. C. Julian, who had purchased a very large deposit of low-grade lead in the canyon for promotion and resale. His reputation already was suspect because of oil stock shenanigans at Signal Hill in the Los Angeles Basin.

About the time mining began, Julian sub-divided the Leadfield townsite and constructed a first class road from Beatty, the nearest railroad connection. With radio and newspaper advertise-ments in California, he drummed up interest in the new development by announcing that a special train would run from Los Angeles in March 1926. On the first day of spring, the twelve Pullmans, two diners, and the passenger car of the "Julian Special" pulled into Beatty, where about a hun-dred waiting automobiles whisked the crowd to the townsite. In all, more than 1100 people at-tended a buffet luncheon with live entertainment provided by a six piece jazz band from Los Angeles. Many had motored in from Tonopah, Goldfield and Las Vegas.

Leadfield in March 1926 promised to be a rich mining district of several thousand population—if contemporary newspapers were to be believed.

The fanfare kicked off a real boom. Chugging autos carrying mining supplies rushed into Lead-field and the settlers located thousands of pros-pects. Other eager fortune hunters invested in Julian's newly formed Western Lead Company which owned the principal properties. The short-lived Leadfield *Chronicle* extravagantly claimed that great ore tonnages soon would be shipped.

That same spring the camp acquired a few businesses, several wooden bunkhouses and a scattering of tent and frame houses. A telephone line was extended across the barren sage from Beatty, and by June enough people lived in Lead-field to establish a post office. On its opening day about 200 people had letters.

But late that summer everything folded be-cause the lead attained values of only low-grade. Leadfield had mined more stockholders' pockets than mountains. By January 1927 only one person remained and the post office closed. Since then the district has been dormant and only a few scattered rusting corrugated iron shacks and con-crete foundations are left. Numerous deep test holes have blemished the canyonsides.

CHLORIDE CLIFF (Chloride City), 13 miles by graded road west of US 95 at a point 7 miles south of Beatty. There is a steep grade the last half mile to the site.

Limited silver mining began in this shallow basin along the crest of the Funeral Mountains as early as 1873, making Chloride Cliff one of Death Valley's oldest developments. The early name for it was "The Franklin Mines." Despite marauding Indians and the remoteness, a few settlers built a road from here to the modern Barstow area by way of Wingate Wash, providing Death Valley with one of its first outlets to civilization. The limited mining ceased before the decade ended.

Development resumed early in this century and during a revival in the spring of 1916 the camp consisted of a blacksmith shop, an assay office, a cookhouse, a bunkhouse, and the superintendent's house. A newly erected cyanide mill operated briefly on lead-silver ores before shutting down by summer, and very little work was done thereafter. A few wooden houses and mill foundations mark the site.

LEE, 14 miles southwest of US 95 at a point 14 miles south of Beatty.

The Lee district initially attracted attention in the spring of 1906 when prospectors found low-grade lode and placer gold atop the east flank of the Funeral Range. A tent camp soon formed below the discoveries. During the height of the Death Valley mining boom in the spring of 1907, a platted townsite (which straddled the state line) numbered several stores, tents, an express office and a post office that had opened in early March. "Lee is coming up big," proclaimed the contemporary press. The local *Herald* began weekly publication and telephone lines were extended to here. But later that year Lee was no longer a place of promise and the camp folded. The post office closed in 1912. Some ore was shipped later, especially in the 1930's. Only mine ruins remain.

————————

Other ghost towns in the Beatty area are: GOLD CENTER, a railroad town 3 miles south of Beatty; CARRARA, 9 miles south of Beatty and the site of an extensive marble quarrying operation from 1913 until 1924; LEELAND, a Tonopah & Tidewater railroad station for several years after 1906; TRANSVAAL, 14 miles east of Beatty, a gold camp with newspapers, several stores and shallow veins in the spring of 1906; and PIONEER, a town of 1000 back in 1909. See the author's *Nevada Ghost Towns & Mining Camps*, available at many bookstores, for history, old pictures and full directions to these and many other forgotten mining camps.

Old STOVEPIPE WELL, 3 miles north of State Route 190 at a point 7 miles east of Stove Pipe Wells Village.

Named for a length of stovepipe pushed down about five feet into a well of brackish water, Stovepipe Well was initially an important Death Valley waterhole for 19th century prospectors. The pipe served as a marker, since wind-blown sand often covered the trail to the water. In the unknown past—probably early in this century—a settler built a one-room dugout with five-foot walls of mud and beer bottles at this famous crossroad.

After 1905-06 when stages to and from Rhyolite began crossing Death Valley to reach Ballarat and Skidoo, Stovepipe Well included a large canvas store, a small tent lodging house, and a tent saloon to quench the traveler's thirst. Cots installed in the bottle house provided extra-cool lodgings; but with area mining on the decline after about 1908, Stovepipe Well reverted to a mere campground.

Envisioning Death Valley as a winter resort, pioneer southern Californian "Bob" Eichbaum in 1926 planned to build desert accommodations here. He projected the grading of a nearly forty-mile toll road from Darwin Wash, past Panamint Valley through Towne Pass and into Death Valley with Stovepipe Well as the eastern terminus. But Eichbaum encountered difficulties in completing the last few miles to the well, so he built his cabins six miles to the west. This was the valley's first resort. At its entrance was the tollgate where Eichbaum collected two dollars for each auto and an additional fifty cents for each passenger.

After Eichbaum's death, Inyo County purchased the road and eventually it was made part of State Route 190. Wells were successfully drilled in the late 1940's. The resort ultimately developed into today's modern Stove Pipe Wells Village, complete with a service station, a cafe, a store, and a motel. Of old Stovepipe Well only some broken glass and a historical marker remain.

In 1906 Stovepipe Station, forty feet below sea level, had the usual simple desert accommodations for both man and beast. Horses were fed and watered and the traveler secured both lodging and a plate of warm food in the canvas hostel. Between the tent and the corral is a merchant's one-horse cart with an umbrella over the seat. The Grapevine Mountains are in the background. The builder of the simple house (below) is not known; some early Death Valley dweller excavated an 18 x 12 foot cellar and built walls of beer bottles held together by layers of mud. The roof consisted of timbers covered by a tarp and finally topped by several inches of dirt. Its interior provided cool lodgings for many a desert traveler.

SCOTTY'S CASTLE, 33 miles north of State Route 190 at a point 9 miles east of Stove Pipe Wells Village or 18 miles north of Furnace Creek Ranch.

Probably the second most famous residence in North America (the Hearst Castle is more popular), Scotty's Castle was named for a publicity loving extrovert named Walter "Death Valley" Scott. The ample backing of A. M. Johnson provided all of the capital for construction; Scotty's reputedly famous hidden gold mine added only controversy, though it helped build the folklore of Scotty.

Kentucky-born Scotty's first job in the West was as a wrangler at Wells, Nevada in the early 1880's. From there he helped drive cattle to southern California but by 1885 he served as a swamper on twenty mule teams hauling borax out of the Harmony Works (see page 8). From 1890 until 1902 he worked in the East and in Europe as a trick rider in Buffalo Bill's Wild West show.

For the rest of his life he resided in Death Valley and in the Mojave Desert where he built his legend as a prospector and owner of a fabulous gold mine. Scotty gained instant fame in July 1905 when he charted the "Coyote Special" and made a 45 hour speed run from Los Angeles to Chicago.

That run, a record until the mid-1930's, remains among history's all-time publicity stunts.

The castle itself was built during 1925-1931 at a cost in excess of a million dollars (perhaps $1.5 million according to its builder, Matt Ray Thompson). Materials were shipped on the Tonopah & Tidewater Railroad to Bonnie Claire, Nevada, and then hauled by trucks to Grapevine Canyon.

Water was piped from Grapevine Springs, one mile distant, and a solar heater provided hot water for the several kitchens and bathrooms in the main house. In the two-story living room Johnson installed a colorful fountain and a fish pond. Water-filled pots hanging from the ceiling and a rock wall with a constant trickle of water cooled the interior. Another room housed a huge pipe organ. Johnson elaborately furnished the hallways and the bedrooms with rugs from Majorca and Florentine leather draperies.

Scotty himself lived at the nearby Lower Grapevine Ranch but moved into the castle just prior to his death in 1954, at age 81. Thereafter the castle was opened for guided tours. For a nominal entrance fee they are available hourly in season and on demand at other times.

Buildings of Scotty's Castle, with their warm-toned walls and dusty-red tiles, are a free adaptation of provincial Spanish architecture. In front of the castle is an unfinished swimming pool. Burly and gregarious Walter "Death Valley" Scott, with his blue eyes, winning grin and bulging waist-line, always had a good story to tell. Easily the West's most famous prospector, Scotty owned no mine but instead relied upon a shy and retiring "partner" for stakes.

A contemporary newspaper reported that Skidoo "grew in a flat little hollow but it did not nestle because a mining camp does not nestle. Like a tin can, it lies where it is thrown." Both wood-frame buildings and tents are in this 1907 view. The stoutness of Skidoo's telephone poles stood as a warning to evil-doers.

SKIDOO, 7 miles east then north of the Emigrant Canyon-Trona road at a point 10.5 miles south of its junction with State Route 190. (27 miles in all from Stove Pipe Wells Village.)

While enroute to Harrisburg early in 1906, two veteran Nevada prospectors—Harry Ramsey and "One-Eye" Thompson—got lost in a rare Death Valley fog six miles north of their destination and found gold-bearing ledges. The contemporary press described the site as at the top of the Panamint Range "where the western wall of Death Valley fades off into thin air." News that respected Rhyolite mining magnate Bob Montgomery had paid an alleged $100,000 cash for several locations, brought an influx of prospectors and miners to Skidoo in mid-1906. Numerous saloonmen and storekeepers quickly set up shop, and nearby Harrisburg was quickly emptied of its inhabitants. Mail and express stage routes from both east and west began running to the camp. The Skidoo post office opened in October 1906.

In a phrase of that era, "23-skidoo" meant "scram." As the story goes, the town acquired its unusual name because the nearest adequate water supply was 23 miles away, over rough terrain in the direction of Telescope Peak. Montgomery soon put in an eight inch pipe line from Telescope to bring water to the burgeoning camp.

By the spring of 1907 Skidoo had more than 500 restless souls, a school, a lively weekly—the *News*, stores, saloons, a bank, and a humming "red light" district. Telephone and telegraph service were extended across Death Valley from Rhyolite. Choice lots sold for as much as $1,000 each until

the era of promotion ended late in 1907, when the nation-wide financial panic put the skids under Skidoo. Beginning the next year the Skidoo Mines Company made it a one-company camp that had produced more than $1.5 million in gold by 1917, when operations ceased and the post office closed. A local 15-stamp mill with a cyanide plant treated the ore.

On a Sunday morning in April 1908 a murder enraged the camp and led to the lynching of the killer. A drifter named "Hootch" Simpson unsuccessful in robbing the Skidoo Bank (located in a store), returned three hours later waving his gun and shouting obscenities. He deliberately shot the unarmed Jim Arnold, one of the camp's most popular men. The sheriff took Simpson into custody, but on Wednesday night a group of armed men entered the jail, seized the prisoner and hanged him from a telephone pole.

After a coroner's inquest had examined the body the next day, the finding was that he had died of strangulation by persons unknown. Simpson was promptly buried, but early Friday morning a Los Angeles *Herald* reporter arrived to cover the story. To avoid disappointing the visitor, the sympathetic and generous Skidoovians obligingly exhumed Simpson and hanged him again, so that he could be photographed.

Small revivals came in later years. A 25-ton cyanide plant in nearby Emigrant Canyon treated ore mined in the late 1930's. No structures remain at Skidoo; a few fallen buildings, the ruins of a wind-torn stamp mill, mine portals and a few graves are left at the Skidoo mine above and west.

HARRISBURG, 2 miles east of the Emigrant Canyon-Trona road at a point 13 miles south of its junction with State Route 190.

Veteran prospectors "Shorty" Harris of Bullfrog fame and French Basque "Pete" Aguereberry passed through the east (upper) edge of Harrisburg Flat early on July 4, 1905 while on their way to the annual Independence Day blowout at Ballarat. The "Basco's" keen eye caught an interesting cropping of free gold which later was traced to the Eureka mine. Aguereberry and Harris shared the fruits of the discovery equally, but after they staked claims and had them recorded, playboy Harris sold out and squandered his money on "Oh Be Joyful" and other liquors.

Because Harris' loose tongue raved about the find, a rush to the site followed in the same week. By September a tent town of 300 or more, initially called Harris*berry*, thrived around the new development which commanded attention until early in 1906 when the sensational Skidoo discoveries lured everyone away. Marking the site are mill ruins, dugouts and cabins of Pete Aguereberry, who struggled to make a living mining low-grade ore until his death in 1945.

From nearby Aguereberry Point, five miles east, it is possible to see both 14,500 foot Mount Whitney, the tallest point in the adjacent United States, and the nation's lowest point, near Badwater, seventy miles east and 282 feet below the sea.

WILDROSE SPRING, alongside the Emigrant Canyon-Trona road at a point 21.5 miles south of its junction with State Route 190.

In the 19th century an adobe stage station operated near this frequently used spring at the lower end of Wildrose Canyon, and a mining boom got underway during the height of Death Valley's frenzy over minerals in 1906-1907. Nearby mining town newspapers ran imaginative two-color advertisements with a red rose overlaying the information about the mining company. But narrow tunneling failed to expose any large vein, though antimony was shipped from the Wildrose mine during World War I. The deposit had been discovered in the 1870's but had not been developed because of its remoteness and insufficient demand for antimony. A picnic ground now occupies the site.

Near the head of Wildrose Canyon is this row of ten gigantic thirty-foot kilns built in 1877 as part of the mining operations in the Lookout (or Modoc) district, twenty miles west. In these 25 foot "beehives" charcoal was made, an agent used in the smelting of lead ores. Each kiln's low-arched entrance and back window had tight fitting iron doors that were sealed after pinyon pine logs had been stocked through both openings. Once set on fire, the wood was allowed to smoulder slowly, so that charcoal would be made. Small holes around the kiln base provided draft. This set of kilns may be the largest and best preserved of its kind in the West.

Blue-eyed and golden-haired Frank "Shorty" Harris was a very small man with front teeth capped with shiny gold. He was a veteran of mining stampedes at Tombstone, Butte and at Coeur d' Alene. In the Death Valley country he co-discovered Bullfrog, where Rhyolite later sprang up, and also shared in the initial finds of the Harrisburg district. One of the Valley's most genial and entertaining liars, "Shorty" died penniless in 1934. His body rests on the floor of Death Valley, with a marker bearing his self-written epitaph, "Here lies Shorty Harris, a single-blanket jackass prospector."

Situated at the base of the vividly streaked Panamint Range, Ballarat and its many adobe houses blend with the earth from which they came, in full retreat from former occupancy to mere memories.

BALLARAT, 3.5 miles east of the Emigrant Canyon-Trona road at a point 38.5 miles south of its junction with State Route 190.

Initial activity in the area started at Post Office Spring, a quarter mile south. In 1849 westbound emigrants stopped there, and in the next year a government survey party also used the water. According to "reliable legend" the spring got its name in the early 1870's during the Panamint boom. Outlaws would emerge from nearby hideouts and deposit outgoing mail in a box attached to a mesquite tree, which certain stage drivers would handle going in and out of Panamint. They also took cash and brought back provisions and mail. In the 1880's prospectors who combed the west flank of the Panamint Range camped at the spring, and a store and blacksmith shop were opened in the early 1890's.

When the Ratcliff and other nearby mines were being worked later in the 1890's, it was decided to lay out a town to allow for ample growth of the area. The forty-acre townsite at the mouth of Pleasant Canyon took the name Ballarat after a famous Australian gold district. Two saloons and a store quickly set up shop. A justice of the peace was appointed, and in July 1897 a post office began to serve the village. Eventually a school opened, as well as a two-story hotel and a boarding house. Stages and freight lines from Darwin and Johannesburg began regular service to the town.

Before the 19th century ended, Ballarat, with about 400 or 500 people, was a busy regional supply center for all nearby camps and mines of the Panamint Range, reportedly "crawling with prospectors and miners." Men from the mines at Argus and Slate Ridge also found a change of pace in Ballarat's hash houses and seven gin shops. Stores, livery and blacksmith shops also had opened. The mild winter climate annually attracted ragged prospectors from California, Nevada and distant mining camps who gathered here to renew old hardships.

Ballarat's decline began in 1905 when the Ratcliff mine suspended operations. The town finally folded around the time of World War I, and the post office closed in September 1917. At Ballarat the famous "Shorty" Harris, co-discoverer of Bullfrog and Harrisburg, spent his last years until his death in 1934. "Seldom Seen Slim" also lived out his life here before passing in 1968. Today the town has a few dwellings, a cemetery, and adobe walls.

PANAMINT CITY, 11 miles northeast of Ballarat ghost town by road and trail.

Though prospectors ventured into the canyons of the bold west flank of the Panamint Range in the early 1860's and organized the Telescope mining district, no rich lodes were found until perhaps 1872, when a gang of robbers found both high-grade silver and a refuge from northern Nevada lawmen in Surprise Canyon. Its steep narrow sides made it possible for an ambush at nearly every turn. Early in the winter of 1873 a silver discovery, said to be worth more than $2,500 a ton by three tenacious prospectors in search of the Lost Gunsight lode, brought about the formation of the Panamint mining district in February of that same year.

Panamint's pioneers camped in caves and rough stockades with bough roofs. Late in 1873 locators showed off bags of silver ore in the pueblo town of Los Angeles to bring attention to the new Death Valley mines. In San Francisco, one locator found a sympathetic ear in Nevada Senator John P. Jones, who just the year before had amassed a fortune in the mining stock of companies owning the fantastic "Big Bonanza" on Virginia City's Comstock Lode.

The news that Jones and Nevada's other Senator, William Stewart, bought several claims from outlaws for a reported $350,000 soon interested delirious investors who envisioned Panamint being another Comstock. The silver senators consolidated their holdings with a stock capitalization of $2 million. Roads to Panamint soon were crowded with all types of rigs, including mule-drawn freighters, buckboards, footpackers and horsemen. The Los Angeles *Star* made notable mention of this new mining excitement, and the editor at Pioche, Nevada said, "The fever is raging. A great many Piochers have already gone and more are preparing to go."

By early 1874 numerous stone huts and pine cabins lined Surprise Canyon for about a mile. The camp quickly became notorious for lawlessness. Sporting "enough guns to stock a hardware store," thieves with wide-brimmed hats and trousers tucked into boots, strolled the main street, buying and selling anything and talking about bullion. Everyone in this restless crowd—grizzly prospectors, painted girls from San Francisco's Barbary coast, enterprising merchants, boisterous wheeler-dealers, laborers and sharp speculators—were on the "pick up", i.e. would not allow a day to pass without making something. One man

Jones and Stewart's twenty-stamp mill and furnace had a forty-ton daily capacity. Initially, ore was brought to the mill by pack train and later by a wire tramway. (The mules in the picture are hauling barrels of water.) The thundering fall of the stamps and the clatter of ponderous machinery constantly echoed through Surprise Canyon, reminding everyone of the bullion being produced. The mill's grey smoke clouds caused no pollution problem in the town because of a prevailing southerly Death Valley breeze. The big mill finally fell silent in May 1877 after a decline in mining at Panamint. Below is the upper part of town in 1875. Several of the frame buildings were used both as a business and a dwelling. A lumberyard, stores and restaurants are shown.

made $10,000 in three months selling gin; another $2,000 in one night playing poker; another a small fortune selling sagebrush lots at $100 to $300 each.

At its height later in 1874, Panamint had perhaps 2000 hustling citizens. More than a dozen saloons and a brewery thrived amid many stores. The tabloid Panamint *News* began tri-weekly publication in November, extolling the rich lodes. For many supply wagons the steep canyon grade into town was insurmountable, so mules and burros often packed supplies into camp, and highgrade ore out. The town butcher owned one of the few large wagons that could make the trip up the canyon. Frequently he had to unload a quarter of beef to haul a stiff to the town's cemetery in Sourdough Canyon.

To overcome Panamint's isolation and to haul out ore, Senator Stewart actually started building a railroad from Los Angeles. Wells, Fargo & Company, the banker and bullion carrier for most other Nevada and eastern California mining camps, had refused to carry bullion from Panamint for fear of robbery by the numerous highwaymen living near the camp. The idea that finally foiled the robbers was to cast the silver bullion into enormous cannonballs that weighed 750 pounds. One time road agents did attempt a robbery of the weighty balls from the mill but failed

and rode away, "frustrated and as mad as hornets." This silver regularly left the camp in unguarded freight wagons.

But Panamint was not destined to be anything as great as the Comstock. Though the 20-stamp silver mill and smelter of the Nevada Senators was blown in during June 1875, most veins were mere "pipes" that extended but a few feet from a shaft in any direction. High freight and milling costs combined to speed the decline and a subsequent exodus early in the fall of 1875. Panamint mining stocks that had been capitalized at several million plummeted on the San Francisco mining exchange. The newspaper stopped publishing in October and was moved to nearby Darwin.

As if taking a clue from these unfortunate circumstances, the elements leagued together in July 1876 to produce a cloudburst high in Surprise Canyon and a flash flood. It carried many of Panamint's abandoned and occupied buildings down the canyon and also damaged the road into the camp. A few people stayed on, though dampened in spirit, and the post office remained until the spring of 1895. There were sporadic revivals in the 20th century, including one in 1925 that used modern machinery. Total district production reached about $2.5 million. Mill walls with the stack of a smelter dominate the townsite.

Colorful in name, location and history, Calico was southern California's most important mining excitement. High transportation charges and a scarcity of water and fuel have plagued mining efforts here. In the mid-1930's Calico was a dead camp, as shown here.

COPPER CITY, 37 miles north of Barstow.

The first strikes were made in the 1880's and during the next decade this camp of a few hundred near Pilot Knob attained its peak of activity. After other ore discoveries in 1907, many mining camp followers took the new Tonopah & Tidewater Railroad to Silver Lake and then rushed here. The revival lasted less than a year. Abandoned shafts, tin cans, and stone walls mark the site which now is inaccessible because it lies within the boundaries of the Naval Ordinance Test Station.

COOLGARDIE, 19 miles north of Barstow.

After initial discoveries in the early 1900's, placer gold fields were worked spasmodically for the next few decades. Various operators used dry washers and concentrators to recover the gold, because there was not enough water to operate a wet-concentrating mill. Little of interest remains.

GOLDSTONE, 33 miles north of Barstow.

Though the first finds came in the early 1880's, no boom developed until high-grade gold was discovered south of Goldstone Lake in December 1915. Leasers began working the lodes during the following spring after ore samples were displayed in a store in Barstow. In the 1920's large mining interests using modern machinery developed the Goldstone, Belmont and Red Bridge mines, with some ore assaying $200 a ton. The camp died just before World War II.

CALICO, 3 miles north of Interstate-15 at Ghost Town Road exit, midway between Barstow and Yermo.

Roving prospectors first found silver on the south slope of the Calico Mountains in 1875, and five years later newly found ore discoveries worth $400 to $500 per ton brought about a small rush and the filing of many claims. In the spring of 1881 came the discovery of the Silver King, Calico's richest mine. By early 1882 a few hundred people supported several businesses on a commercial street flanked by tents and adobe buildings on a narrow mesa between Wall Street and Odessa Canyons. The weekly Calico *Print* appeared in October and a local 10-stamp mill began to work the ores. But in the spring of 1883 most of the local miners forsook Calico when borax was discovered three miles east at Borate.

Later in 1883 a fire destroyed much of the camp, but it boomed the next year and quickly attained a population that some say reached 2500. In addition to about two dozen saloons and gam-bling dives that never closed, Calico also had aspects of a larger city, including a dancing school, a church, a public school and a literary society. As a result of consolidations, the mines were worked systematically after 1884. Late in 1888 the Oro Grande Mining Company erected a $250,000 60-stamp mill on the north bank of the Mojave River near Daggett and connected it with the Silver King mine by the ten mile narrow-gauge Calico Railroad, completed that same year.

Virtually all of the mines closed in the early 1890's, when the price of silver declined, and the narrow-gauge was dismantled just after the turn of the century. Around 1917 a cyanide plant built here recovered values from the Silver King mine dumps, and another small revival occurred in the early 1930's.

By 1935 the camp was abandoned after at least $13 million (some say $20 million) in silver had been mined. In 1950 Knott's Berry Farm in Buena Park bought the townsite and began restorations. Its owner, Walter Knott, as a young man helped build a silver mill here at the time of World War I. One of the attractions is the one-mile short line "Calico & Odessa" railroad which loops through steep canyons and hills past old mines and buildings north of Calico. The original townsite has been obliterated completely by the new buildings.

BORATE, via unimproved roads, 6.5 miles north then west of Interstate-15 at Mineola exit, 4 miles east of Yermo.

When borax was found three miles east of Calico in 1883, a rush developed to Mule Canyon and other parts of the Calico Mountains to locate 20-acre claims of borax deposits. The William T. Coleman & Company soon bought the most important properties, but no mining was started until after "Borax" Smith acquired them in 1890.

With the Atlantic & Pacific Railroad (Santa Fe Railroad after 1897) only about ten miles below the borax mines, Smith centered his operations here in the high desert and abandoned all of his Death Valley fields. A small camp formed that had a post office after July 1896. Late in 1898 the eleven mile narrow-gauge Borate & Daggett Railroad began hauling ore to the Santa Fe Railroad depot at Daggett, this displacing the dust-covered strings of mule teams and a short-lived steam tractor. But in 1907, with higher costs encountered in deeper mining, operations were abandoned in favor of the Lila C. mine at Ryan. Some mine ruins are left.

1407.

The camp of Borate, shown at right around 1900, was a rude collection of wooden buildings scattered amid mine dumps. As an animal team leaves the camp (top, opposite page) and descends the steep canyon, it is necessary for the teamster to leave his customary position on the left wheel horse and sit atop the ore wagon to man the brake. The jerkline which extends from the teamster's hand to the left lead horse, and the dust-covered chain, are clearly shown.

Before 1900 "Borax" Smith unsuccessfully tried to supplant the long-line mule teams with this oil burning high-wheeled steam tractor. It saw only limited service in 1894 hauling borax from the Borate mine to the railroad station at Daggett. This tractor, nicknamed "Old Dinah," was only slightly faster than the animal teams and could haul a larger load, but it proved to be unmanageable in the crooked canyons below Borate. In about 1903 the Keane Wonder mine purchased the tractor to make hauls eastward over Daylight Pass. On the first trip the tractor dug itself into the sandy road; it sat in the hot sun for nearly thirty years before it was brought to its final resting place at Furnace Creek Ranch.

Until the railroad was built to the Borate mine in 1898, borax was regularly hauled to Daggett by animal teams. The wagons were run up on high platforms to facilitate ore transfers to Santa Fe railroad box cars. The product was then hauled to the Pacific Coast Borax Company's refinery at Alameda on San Francisco Bay.

Hints for Desert Travel

By staying on paved highways and excellent graded roads, tourists can easily visit several Death Valley ghost towns in a modern low-centered car. Though you will not need camp gear, *always* carry water or some other liquid and blankets to minimize discomfort in the event of a breakdown. If any trouble develops stay with the car, because a ranger on patrol likely will be with you before you can walk out for help. Your headlights are a night signaling device.

Many other interesting ghost towns and mines are reached only by venturing into isolated back country on primitive roads. Preparation for a desert trip such as this begins at home. A definite must is a food and water supply equal to at least a gallon per person for each day you expect to be away from a town or settlement. Avoid glass containers.

The following supplies may be helpful: sleeping bags, a gas stove, a portable ice box, non-glass water containers, canteens for hiking, several changes of loose-fitting garments, hats, gloves, a raincoat, a first-aid kit and book, flares for emergency use, maps and literature, sunglasses, blankets, matches, compass. Keep your equipment simple and portable.

A well-equipped desert-bound auto should include: tools, shovels, flashlights, burlap bags or a tire pump, a gasoline can, and a tire jack.

Before leaving home, make sure that your car is in top mechanical condition. Clean and flush the engine's cooling system. Check for cooling leaks. Be sure that the fanbelt and radiator hoses are in good condition.

At the last service station before embarking on a back road, fill to the brim with gasoline and check the oil. The tires and the spare should be properly inflated. Clean the radiator core of bugs and debris that might restrict air flow. Since a flash flood or storm can change the terrain overnight, ask a ranger about the condition of unimproved roads in the Monument and heed his advice. For an extended trip on back roads, it is well to travel in two-car parties or tell someone your itinerary. Be sure to give notice of your return!

Carry at least five gallons of water for the radiator, though special radiator water tanks are situated along strategic points on the main paved highways.

Once on an unimproved road, keep a written record of mileages and significant landmarks. Watch the fuel gauge; it is easy to misjudge gas consumption while driving in lower gears.

Always keep your wheels on the road. Making your own trail is illegal in the Monument. Watch for high centers or rocks on the road that your car cannot clear. Always make camp on high ground. Never park your car in a wash or a depression where an uphill run must be made to get out. Park on a slope, so that you can coast to get started in case the ignition fails.

Learn to use the engine as a brake on long downgrades where repeated brake applications might heat the brake linings, causing them to fail or lose efficiency. Downshift as you descend. Drive upgrades in low gear; your engine will overheat if you labor a car in high gear. On grades the climbing car has the right-of-way. If you are descending on a narrow road and you see or hear another car coming, yield to it by stopping at a turnout and waiting until it passes.

Never hurry! Gullies, sharp ascents from washes, or any other pitches in the road must be taken slowly. It is easy to damage an oil pan or transmission by striking the road or a flying rock while driving fast on uphill grades. After crossing dust zones test the brakes.

Driving Emergencies

When STUCK IN THE SAND, stop the car immediately. Survey the situation; decide whether to go forward or back out. Partially deflate the tires for more traction. Make a brush or burlap roadway (a hub cap can be used for a shovel). Jack up the rear end and place rocks underneath. Never crawl under the car when it is jacked up! Have someone stand on the rear bumper for additional weight on the wheels. Then ease out. Rock the car forward and backward until it is moving a few feet at a time, then drive off slowly to keep the wheels from spinning. When in sand, steer straight in available ruts and drive steadily. If you turn sharply or accelerate suddenly, you will get stuck.

46

Cool an OVERHEATED ENGINE by turning the car into the wind. Do not stop the motor. Pour water over the front of the radiator core. Do *not* remove the radiator cap unless the gauge shows that the water has cooled. Then fill the radiator and proceed.

If the ENGINE WILL NOT START, look for several things. You may be out of gas. A line may be punctured, causing loss of fuel. Or the carburetor may be flooded. Let the car sit for a full minute. Then push the accelerator to the floor and hold it there while again trying the starter.

Look for loose battery terminal connections or corroded terminals. Clean and tighten them. Or a high tension wire may be loose. Give it a gentle push into its socket in the distributor cap. Check spark plug wires and tighten any that are loose.

If the car comes to a bucking halt while driving in hot weather, especially in high altitudes, you have encountered vapor lock. Raise the hood and let the engine cool. Place a wet cloth on the fuel pump. Wait ten to fifteen minutes before starting the engine; repeated efforts to restart will run the battery down.

Desert Perils

EXPOSURE. While in the desert be prepared for hot and cold weather in extremes. Always wear a hat and sunglasses. Avoid removing your shirt; do not wear shorts. Clothing should be adequate to ward off the sun's hot rays and also retain body heat during cool nights. Avoid excessive activity in the midday sun to avoid heat exhaustion or sunstroke.

HEAT EXHAUSTION often results from dehydration or prolonged exposure to the sun. Symptoms are a headache, weakness, dizziness and a clammy colorless skin. Lay him in the shade, loosen his clothing and give him salt water about a teaspoon to a quart. *The victim continues to sweat.*

SUNSTROKE is very serious. Symptoms include nausea, dizziness, irritableness and a weak feeling. *The victim stops sweating.* Simultaneously, his skin becomes hot, dry and red, and his pulse rate increases. Since the body temperature rises far above normal, *get the victim to a doctor.* In the meanwhile, lower body temperature by splashing the victim with cold water and wrapping him in wet sheets or clothing. Place his forearms in cold water containers or place ice cubes on each wrist. Apply ice or cold cloths to his hands and fan him. Massage his legs upward toward the heart. If conscious, give him salt water or other drinks but no stimulants.

The bites of SPIDERS and SCORPIONS found in California may cause considerable discomfort but rarely death. Neither comes to bite you in bed, though during the night they might crawl into your blankets to keep warm, biting you after you roll over. Contrary to belief the hairy TARANTULA is not poisonous, but do not tease him.

Everyone exploring in the desert should keep on the alert for RATTLESNAKES. Since many myths have been perpetuated about snakes, it is well to learn the facts. They *will* strike without a signal. For concealment and comfort, they prefer early morning and evening shadows and lower temperatures. Rattlesnakes will not provoke a fight; they prefer to remain in hiding unless startled or angered.

Be on the lookout for snakes in any hilly area, especially in washes containing damp soil and shade. When you see small rodents, you are in snake country. Inside old mines and pits, the areas under boards or fallen logs and loose bark, and beneath ledges of rock are typical snake hangouts. Never handle a snake even if it appears to be dead. Always be mindful where you place your hands and feet; do not forget to look at the ground as you get out of your car. When gathering wood or searching through debris, wear long gloves and high boots and use a garden tool.

Gather firewood and make camp before sunset and avoid hiking after the sun goes down. Do not camp near brush, a wood pile or a rocky slope. The best protection is common sense and a keen eye.

If you should be bitten, keep calm and avoid unnecessary activity. Apply a tourniquet above the wound, pack it in ice or water soaked cloths, and *get to a doctor.* The tourniquet, which should be loose enough to insert a finger under it, should be unfastened briefly about every half hour. Consult your first aid manual for further instructions, if help is not available within a reasonable time—about eight hours for an adult. In that case, the most effective treatment is an "X" shaped incision of each fang mark and suction.

Watch for Overexertion

Travel at a leisurely pace. Use the morning and late afternoon for exploring and find a shady spot during midday to rest. Exhaustion comes easily in the mining areas because of high altitudes. Do not overdo anything; traveling and hiking have their limits.

Food needs are the same in the desert as back home, so do not try to live on fruit and candy. Eat a big breakfast and go light on food intake until evening. Throughout the day drink plenty of water. Often the dry air reaches into the pores and dries sweat before it has time to wet the skin.

Above all, never venture into abandoned mines and excavations! Amateurs cannot judge the strength of tunnel walls and roofs and the quality of timbering. Avoid any curious peering into open mine shafts; a cave-in may result from a person's weight on the edge of the shaft. Also watch your pets and children in the vicinity of open pits and shafts. Camp far from old excavations.

Respect private property, whether it is mine equipment at patented claims or household items in a desert home.

Even summer trips into high areas in The Monument can be pleasant. Often it is only around 100 degrees in the daytime, and even higher temperatures can be quite bearable because of the low humidity. The west slope of the Panamint Range is ideal for extended summer hikes and ghost-towning. October-November and February-March are the best times to explore in the Monument. Winter days are sunny and warm, but the nights can be quite cold.

Survival

Avoiding tragedy in emergency situations depends more on knowledge and a will to survive than on survival supplies. The biggest danger is dehydration. When trapped in back territory, conserve body moisture by keeping adequately clothed and by drinking water. The base of cliffs, the lowest points of dry stream beds, or any thickly planted area may be sources of water. A radiator drained of anti-freeze is an emergency supply of drinking water.

If you are on an unimproved road and decide to walk out for help, leave on the steering wheel a note indicating the time you left your car and the direction you are headed. Many abandoned cars have been found by a rescue posse which had no idea where to begin looking for the owner. Drink water before leaving the car and begin your walk in the early morning or evening. Carry water and dress for protection against the extremes of desert temperatures. Seek shade during midday. Never travel in a storm. Find a shelter and keep your back to the wind. Desert distances are deceptive; mountains and other landmarks appear closer than they really are.

. . . And Finally

A list of regulations governing Death Valley National Monument is available at the Furnace Creek headquarters. Prohibited is any collecting of rocks or plants or picking of wildflowers. Hunting, wounding, capturing, or attempting to capture any wild bird or animal also is prohibited, except in cases where a poisonous snake or a dangerous animal may threaten injury or death.

Please do not deface or destroy road signs, historical ruins, archaelogical remains and geological formations. Fines can result. Firearms may be carried only when cased, sealed or broken down.

Camp in designated areas. Please use the receptacles provided for refuse. Trees may not be cut for campfires; presto logs may be purchased at Furnace Creek Ranch and at Stove Pipe Wells Village. Help keep the roadsides clean by carrying a litter bag. When camping in the back country, please burn trash and either bury or carry unburnable refuse to garbage cans. No one enjoys seeing an untidy camp.

Report anyone in trouble to a ranger or at the nearest settlement. May you have safe and happy desert traveling.

Books About Death Valley

Space limitations forbid the listing of all sources used while writing this volume. Old newspaper files were read by the volume; dozens of out-of-print Death Valley books were read and state and federal documents were consulted. Should anyone be interested in sources of information, documentation will be furnished if an inquiry is sent to the publisher.

Of the dozens of Death Valley books in print, the following are recommended because of their accuracy and general usefulness.

A good overall impression of Death Valley with numerous well selected color illustrations is Bill Clark's *Death Valley, The Story Behind The Scenery* (Las Vegas: KC Publications, 1972). Specific comment on Monument services and recreation with maps to scenic sites is in *Exploring Death Valley* by Ruth Kirk (Stanford: Stanford University Press, 1965).

The book that is required reading and the beginning point for research on any facet of Death Valley and the surrounding eastern California desert area is E.I. Edwards' valuable descriptive bibliography, *The Enduring Desert* (Los Angeles: Ward Ritchie Press, 1969). The Death Valley and Beatty areas had several railroads, and the complete readable story (augmented by rare photographs) is in *Railroads of Nevada & Eastern California, Volume II*, by David F. Myrick (Berkeley: Howell-North Books, 1963). Three Harold Weight publications issued by Calico Press at Twenty nine Palms, each an accurate interesting history, are *Rhyolite* (1953), *Twenty Mule Team Days in Death Valley* (1955), and *Greenwater* (1969).